U
TRAVEL
GUIDE TO
CHARLOTTE
2024

Discovering Charlotte: A Southern Gem's Charms Unveiled

JOSEPH RAY

TABLE OF CONTENTS

CHAPTER 1: WHY GO TO CHARLOTTE

Tucked within the Piedmont region's sleepy rolling hills, this bustling city is anything however a quiet Southern belle. Charlotte, North Carolina, explodes with growing groups, burgeoning sports activities franchises and an evolving culinary scene. Though the Queen City is understood for the Charlotte Motor Speedway and the NASCAR Hall of Fame, it's much extra than a haven for those with a want for pace. Uptown Charlotte – make certain now not to name it downtown – is crawling with suits and travelers, even as artwork aficionados and way of life hounds flood the Plaza Midwood and NoDa (or North Davidson) neighborhoods. Meanwhile, the ones on the lookout for a pint of neighborhood beer might not need to overlook South End, domestic to a handful of the city's top breweries.

This ever-expanding town has a knack for retaining an East Coast tempo with out stomping on its Southern roots; locals are devoted to preserving classic Southern charm alive. The mixing of these two personalities is engagingly lively and romantic.

Charlotte City Attractions

Uptown Charlotte (that is certainly downtown Charlotte) is in which you'll discover the museums:

the Levine Museum of the New South, the Mint Museum Uptown and the youthful ImaginOn are a number of the nearby standouts. For a younger, hip vibe, head to the tattoo parlors and stay song venues of the NoDa arts district, or browse the funky boutiques and eateries in Plaza-Midwood. At the multi-useful EpiCentre in the heart of the town, visitors can discover nightlife, cafes, shops and a rooftop terrace. For top notch unearths at price range prices, buyers will love the Concord Mills shopping mall and the Charlotte Premium Outlets. Cap off your day with a meal and a drink at one of the many craft breweries around town, a gourmet meals truck, a neighborhood farmers' marketplace, or a classic Southern eatery like Midwood Smokehouse.

The Sporting Life

Sixteen NASCAR groups are based totally in and around Charlotte, which is why the NASCAR Hall of Fame and Hendrick Motorsports Complex are top sights on the town. If you want to peer an actual NASCAR race, head to the Charlotte Motor Speedway. There are lots of other professional spectator sports activities that visitors can soak up as nicely: Carolina Panthers soccer, Charlotte Hornets basketball and Carolina Hurricanes hockey.

Get Outdoors

Within the town limits, snatch a picnic lunch and stroll via Freedom Park. Further afield are many opportunities for kayaking, canoeing, river rafting and tubing at locations just like the U.S. National Whitewater Center and Lake Norman. There are also more than 40 golf guides in the greater Charlotte location.

How To Get To Charlotte, NC

Charlotte Douglas International Airport (CLT)

Charlotte has its very own airport the Charlotte Douglas Internationally Airport with each day departures which include nonstop flights to over one hundred sixty destinations. If you're coming from distant places and may't get a right away flight to Charlotte, you may possibly get a connecting flight from both the East Coast or West Coast.

By Car : You can get to Charlotte via using on Interstates seventy seven and 85, or via taking Interstate 40 if you're coming from the West Coast.

Ride share: Taxi services between Charlotte Airport and the city center value an average of $25. Uber and Lyft also operate in cities. You may even take the Sprinter Bus from the airport to Charlotte's Uptown.

Amtrak Train : Amtrak offers 3 routes that join Charlotte from East Coast and West Coast. The Carolinian direction from New York, the Piedmont course from Raleigh, and the Crescent course which connects New York and New Orleans with Charlotte.

By Bus: You also can take a bus from many close by cities together with Richmond and Atlanta. There are services each day with Greyhound buses, in addition to cheaper alternatives like Megabus.

Light Rail: Charlotte's LYNX Blue Line mild rail connects 26 stations. You can get a spherical experience for much less than $five and without problems bounce from one part of the town to some other. Before you go to, you'll need to down load the CATS Pass app so you can purchase your price tag, as well as to preserve track at the bus and rail timetable.

Best Ways To Get Around Charlotte

Charlotte North Carolina light rail transportation shifting gadget

There are many things to do in Charlotte which might be localized to at least one vicinity, however driving by means of vehicle may be the excellent way to explore the entirety.

By vehicle

Charlotte is a car-centric town, and renting a automobile gives the most handy manner to navigate and witness its principal points of interest Uptown and for the duration of its suburbs.

Travelers need to additionally pressure giant distances to coastal destinations like Lake Norman (forty mins from the town middle) and the coast, which might be famous throughout summer.

A private vehicle also makes driving from the city to nearby small cities worth traveling and other major North Carolina cities less complicated. For people with a penchant for long journeys, there is lots greater a laugh to discover in Raleigh, a 2.5-hour power from Charlotte.

Fittingly, numerous condo automobile businesses like Alamo and Hertz anticipate tourists at the Charlotte Douglas International Airport, so locating a hire shouldn't be hard.

Light Rail

For those making plans to explore Charlotte's Uptown and stick with the neighborhoods bordering the metropolis middle, the LYNX mild rail gadget is an first-rate choice to get around. It has 26 stations, and trains cover a 20-mile route with stops at splendid points of interest just like the Discovery Place Science and Mint Museum Uptown.

Fares: $2.20 consistent with ride for adults, seniors, and kids pay discounted fares

Schedule: five:30 am – 1:30 am each day, jogging each 7.Five mins in the course of rush hour and 15 minutes in the course of off-top hours.

A LYNX sprinter car gives passengers free rides, covering around four miles from the city's ancient district in West End to the Elizabeth neighborhood through the city center. With 17 stops between the begin of the adventure to the destination, vacationers need now not worry about lacking their drop-off factors.

By bus

The metropolis's Charlotte Area Transit System (CATS) operates as a minimum 70 buses on nearby, local, and specific routes. These are an exquisite opportunity to the light rail.

Fares: $2.20 in keeping with journey for adults, seniors, and children pay discounted fares

By taxi

Taxis are to be had throughout the town, with most important companies like Yellow Tax Co. And Crown Cab presenting handy rides to visitors. These will be beneficial when visiting points of interest outside Charlotte, consisting of Charlotte Motor Speedway and Whitewater Center, however do not have a condo.

Taxi fees: $2.50 initial price plus $2.5 for each extra mile traveled.

By bike

Charlotte Joy Rides is the town's motorcycle-proportion software, with nearly 350 motorcycles spread across 30 stations, specifically in Uptown.

Things to Do in Charlotte

Charlotte Motor Speedway

Charlotte runs on NASCAR—it is the birthplace of the game—so a go to Charlotte Motor Speedway is a have to whether you're a diehard fan or a amateur. You'll find every kind here, from bankers throwing back beers and women in American flag bikini tops to genuine fans who camp out in hen bone alley. They're proud, and it's very loud, but among the racing and the humans-looking, it is natural entertainment.

Daniel Stowe Botanical Garden

Birds sing, plants bloom, and bees buzz approximately at Daniel Stowe, a 110-acre public botanical lawn. And while it is able to be outdoor of Charlotte right (similar to these awesome day journeys are), it's properly worth the attempt: It's a pleasing area to spend an afternoon, whether you are a diehard inexperienced thumb who wants to spot rare kinds of vegetation and plant life or you simply need to wander off amid a sea of shade for some hours. There are seven themed gardens starting from perennials to four-season gardens, along with a conservatory that homes orchids and tropical plants. If you're here with own family, take a look at out Lost Hollow, the children's garden, which has a sunken pond and play spaces.

Camp North End

Charlotte's Camp North End is a seventy six-acre multi-use space with public artwork, meals stalls, stores, workplaces and extra in a former car manufacturing facility and navy depot. It's a huge complex, but there's continually somewhere to hang around for a chunk (quite literally—you could stretch out in a hammock if that cafe desk and chairs would not in shape your desires). It's all approximately strolling round, absorbing the cool, innovative vibe— and ingesting.

7th Street Public Market

This market bustles with humans sampling the whole thing from crepes to local brews. Ideal for a noon workplace destroy and lazy weekend afternoons over coffee and treats, it is a casual spot for buddies to catch up and just proper for a Saturday night time damage for couples with children in tow. Families love how laid-lower back it is, and it is simply proper for grabbing espresso with a friend or swinging by using earlier than a night time out. It's made for tasting, so come hungry and select your manner through: Start with breakfast at SC Café, followed through dumplings at Momo Station. Nibble on cheese at Orrman's, where there are more than one hundred differing types. There's a lot extra, together with standout coffee that's well worth the experience by myself.

Little Sugar Creek Greenway

Little Sugar Creek Greenway, a network of trails, paved paths, parks, and streams, includes 4 downstream sections in and round Charlotte. When it's complete, it is going to be 19 miles long, and will run all the way all the way down to the South Carolina nation line. It runs from Cordelia Park to just north of Uptown, and it is a paradise for out of doors fanatics. (As is Crowders Mountain State Park, in addition down this listing.) This greenway is designed for walkers, runners, bikers, and stroller-pushing mother and father, however there are benches for folks who want to take a seat and take in the view—and people-watch.

U.S. National Whitewater Center

U.S. National Whitewater Center is the largest man-made whitewater river within the world, and it is also an Olympic education site. But there is a lot more than rapids here; as a substitute, it is a 1,300-acre playground for the whole family. With rock climbing and mountain biking on more than 50 miles of trails, the complex appears like an Outside magazine unfold—right out of doors Charlotte. What you do here relies upon to your pastimes. If you're a river rat, you may love the whitewater rapids; if heights are your component, try the zip lines and rock climbing.

NASCAR Hall of Fame

NASCAR's most well-known racetrack might be in Daytona, but its domestic is Charlotte; in the end, a few of the conventional racers hailed from the hills surrounding the town. Attached to the Charlotte Convention Center, the NASCAR Hall of Fame is a 86,500-rectangular-foot, formidable swoop of a building that recalls the form of a racetrack. Considered greater than a museum, this enjoyment facility is a excessive-tech venue that is extraordinary even for non-NASCAR fanatics. Everything, similar to the game, is oversized and fast, from an interactive card that creates a motive force identification for you, to the "Glory Road" parade of displayed automobiles from famous drivers, to the present keep, which has extra square pictures than a few of the downtown restaurants inside strolling distance of this museum.

Blumenthal Performing Arts Center

Comprising the Belk Theater, Booth Playhouse, and Stage Door Theater, the Blumenthal is floor 0 for way of life in Charlotte. The complicated hosts a huge form of acting arts, which includes dance, classical musical, live theater, and comedy. You'll see large-call stars like Diana Krall and Andy Grammer alongside Broadway shows and poetry slams. The schedule packs plenty of own family-friendly fun, from Frozen for the infants to Blue Man Group for the older children. Art lovers, lifestyle vultures, and every body hoping to affect a friend will adore it right here.

Discovery Place

Colorful, innovative and designed around experiential gaining knowledge of, Charlotte's Discovery Place is the vicinity to maintain youngsters of all ages entertained. Here, you might not be studying placards–you will be studying firsthand. The well-knownshows are interactive and fun, and whilst they're geared for children, adults will revel in it too. There is not any guided tour. This is the form of vicinity in which buyers run to the exhibit that hobbies them the most earlier than shifting on to the following super issue. Discovery Place does not provide a restaurant, however you are in Uptown so there may be usually some thing nearby.

Crowders Mountain State Park

Crowders Mountain State Park is an outdoor enthusiast's paradise. There are 11 trails, canoe rentals to be had, a 9-acre lake prime for fishing, the option to backcountry camp, and the opportunity of mountain climbing and bouldering with a permit. The view from the pinnacle is brilliant. On clean days, you can see for miles and can even spot Charlotte's skyline. Don't permit its name idiot you. Crowders Mountain State Park is a incredible vicinity to break out crowds.

Arts & Science Council: Public Art Walking Tour

This is a self-guided tour, so you can continue at your very own pace. Download a map or listen to the podcast, and you will discover your self traipsing thru all of Uptown to view the general public artwork. You want not anything however a great pair of footwear and your cellphone to navigate the tour. It's unfastened and a pleasant manner to get to know the community. We love Charlotte's museums, however there's not anything quite like artwork it truly is incorporated into the surroundings—it appears like a residing and respiration item.

Lake Norman

Lake Norman, simply 20 miles north of Uptown, feels a million nautical miles away from Charlotte's hustle and bustle. This is the largest man-made lake inside the Carolinas, which means that there may be plenty of area for boating, fishing, watersports, and simply chilling out. You'll see every kind here, from beer-toting and bikini-clad singles to adventurous, amusing-seeking households. Whether you fancy pontoon boats or paddle forums, kayaks or wakeboards, take into account that Lake Norman is all about being on the water—no longer just looking at it from the coastline.

Levine Center for the Arts

The Levine Center for the Arts is not simply one vicinity well worth hitting, it's four: the Bechtler Museum of Modern Art, Harvey B. Gantt Center for African-American Arts + Culture, John S. And James L. Knight Theater, and Mint Museum Uptown. Three of the museums showcase art, history, and way of life; the Knight, in the meantime, is a performance venue. Each group, even though, is worth of an afternoon in its very own right.

Freedom Park

Freedom Park is to Charlotteans what Central Park is to New Yorkers. It's in which they play as kids, feeding the ducks and playing at the swings in the playgrounds, and which they maintain to go to as adults. The 98-acre park, which sits between Charlotte's Dilworth and Myers Park neighborhoods, has a seven-acre lake and facilities for basketball, tennis, volleyball, football, and baseball. But if you'd prefer to throw down a blanket and stare at cloud formations, there are satisfactory patches of grass for lounging around, too.

For those in Charlotte trying to discover a lovely, serene park: Freedom Park is the perfect desire. Check out the 98-acre park placed at 1900 East Boulevard, among Charlotte's historic Dilworth and Myers Park neighborhoods.

Freedom Park is focused on a seven-acre lake, which turns into a warm spot for natural world during the spring and summer time months.

Charlotte, North Carolina, is thought to be a fairly inexperienced metropolis, with many parks and possibilities for people to step out of doors and get lively. Freedom Park is a fantastic vicinity for a stroll, run, or bike using.

For the ones staying in Downtown Charlotte, Freedom Park is three miles faraway from the coronary heart of that place.

Public transportation in Charlotte, NC

At Carowinds, visitors of the town can revel in a exciting, amusing park placed adjoining to Interstate seventy seven in Charlotte, North Carolina. On top of that, Carowinds straddles the North Carolina-South

Carolina nation line, making this a amusing vicinity to revel in both states without delay!

The park functions more than 60 international-class rides, the Carolinas' best waterpark, stay leisure, Camp Snoopy, and down-domestic Carolina cuisine.

Tickets start at $39.Ninety nine for the 'Early Days Deal,' $44.99 for a trendy daylight price tag, $79.99 for a two-day price tag, and $14 according to month for a 12 months-lengthy Silver Pass.

View of downtown Charlotte, North Carolina

Moving into the Uptown vicinity of Charlotte, the Mint Museum is the precise area to spend a day. Here, traffic can explore the property, which houses the across the world renowned Craft + Design collection, in addition to top notch collections of American and cutting-edge artwork.

The museum has regular stay seminars, performances, and opportunities to view global portions, so this can without difficulty end up a favourite forestall all through the holiday.

Mint Museum Uptown takes round 2–three hours to walk via. The exceptional time of the week to peer the museum is for the duration of the weekdays (Monday through Thursday), because it does get extra crowded on weekends.

Tickets: $15 for adults, $10 for seniors, $10 for college students, and $6 for the ones among five and 17 years vintage. Anyone underneath five is available in loose.

Street in Charlotte NC

Another spot to explore in Charlotte is the Belk Theater, located at Blumenthal Performing Arts Center. Blumenthal Performing Arts is a non-profit, multi-venue appearing arts in Charlotte, website hosting many suggests all through the yr. The Belk Theater is the largest venue within the acting arts center, keeping 2,100 human beings.

This complicated opened in 1992 and became committed to the metropolis and the continuation of the humanities. It's also worth noting that there are 4 different theaters in the Blumenthal Performing Arts Center, so travelling the facility ought to take 2+ hours.

Because the Belk Theater is inside the a good deal larger Blumenthal Performing Arts Center, it may be a laugh to excursion the property earlier than or after watching a display. This is the most important theater of the four, so maximum large-call indicates will take area here.

Aerial view of Charlotte, North Carolina

Charlotte has the rare difference of being the birthplace of NASCAR racing, and the Charlotte Motor Speedway is wherein locals and guests converge to experience the velocity spectacle. This is one of the great things to do in Charlotte for journey-seekers!

The ecosystem is nothing brief of electrifying as spectators saturate the air with cheers and jeers all through one of the purest sorts of enjoyment in the metropolis.

Check the internet site to check out scheduled occasions and ticket prices.

Blooming tree in Charlotte, NC

Nature lovers and fanatics will relish a tour of the 110-acre Daniel Stowe Botanical Garden. This inexperienced space is characterized by chirping birds, buzzing bees, and blooming flora, culminating in a completely unique natural space ideal for a relaxed afternoon walk.

The facility homes several rare varieties of regional plant life, ranging from perennial to seasonal plants. Visitors also can view excellent orchids and different tropical vegetation on the on-web page conservatory.

Admissions: Adults $14.95, Seniors (60+) $12.95, Children (2-12) $7.95, Children (Under 2) Free

Hours: Wednesdays to Sundays (10 am – 4 pm)

For the best own family experience, prevent by way of the Lost Hollow, a laugh children's garden with exceptional play regions and a completely unique sunken lawn.

South End Water Tower, Charlotte, NC

Camp North End is a one-of-a-kind outdoor area in Charlotte spanning seventy six acres and capabilities stores, offices, food stalls, public art, and even a former military depot. People from all corners of the metropolis accumulate here to hang around, interact, or check out the numerous agencies in the location.

Window shopping is one of the quality activities in Charlotte, but there is nothing incorrect with choosing up a memento or two either.

Hours: Monday to Sunday (10 am - 10 pm)

Downtown view of Charlotte, NC

The international's biggest synthetic whitewater river, the United States National Whitewater Center is a interesting appeal in Queen City, supplying unadulterated a laugh for the whole own family.

Besides rafting on the rapids, a 1300-acre playground spoils kids and adults with limitless play activities, even as 50 miles of trails on the complicated welcome mountain bikers to gauge their experience.

The web site additionally has a zip line to make sure all visitors have something to waft their boat.

All-Access passes: $seventy five for adults and $65 for kids (nine and more youthful)

Hours: Open day by day 24 hours

Railyard in Charlotte, NC

Charlotte's Museum of History preserves and chronicles the city's in advance days in an eight-acre facility packed with memorabilia. Take a ride down memory lane to the Revolutionary generation on the remains of the Alexander Rock House, which become constructed in 1774.

Six galleries at the campus residence rotating and everlasting reveals comprising artifacts and ancient figures that left an indelible mark on shaping the city's future.

CHAPTER 2: BEST TIME TO VISIT CHARLOTTE

Drone Aerial of Downtown Charlotte, North Carolina, NC, USA

Queen City is lucky to have a temperate weather during the yr, that means vacationers can come each time they want a holiday. The first-rate time to go to Charlotte is within the shoulder seasons, March to May, and September to November, when guests are rewarded with much less crowded streets, greater affordable lodge quotes, and great outdoor weather.

Spring offers an remarkable possibility to plan a Queen City vacation. Although it starts off evolved cold in March, the weather warms to a relaxed eighty one levels Fahrenheit as the season maintains. The time is ideal for roaming the beneficiant open areas inside the city, and a hike or stroll will do nicely to shake off the slight sit back in spring.

Pack enough layers while touring to Charlotte at some point of spring to keep away from the night bloodless and be extra cushty trekking outdoors. A raincoat will also are available in reachable as every month of the season experiences around 10 days of rainfall.

Summertime may be tempting for plenty visitors to Charlotte as this is the busiest visitor season, full of a laugh activities and festivals. Those with a taste for toasty climate descend at the town to experience the 87-diploma conditions. The sun remains up lengthy enough for first-timers to completely witness the sights and sounds of the town, and the situations activate many to cool off on a seashore at Lake Norman or the coast.

However, summer season can be brutally muggy, and the unpredictable Charlotte weather approach the heavens can open anytime without warning. Furthermore, flight and resort fees height because of the high range of tourists, so e book nicely earlier to pass the exorbitant costs.

Bring light and breathable apparel to counter the heat and humidity; shorts, t-shirts, and a suit to splash within the pool. An umbrella will also be accessible for outdoor adventures, as August is the year's wettest month.

Fall is the opposite shoulder season and a first-rate time to vacation in Charlotte. With summer time crowds departing the metropolis and the weather cooling off around mid-October, the setting is good for coming across the metropolis points of interest with out the hustle and bustle of summer season. The lovely fall foliage attracts traffic out of doors, and accommodations costs are a lot better.

The satisfactory time for price range tourists is iciness, as accommodations provide beneficiant discounts and prices drop dramatically. This is the slowest tourism season, with temperatures dipping to lows of 30 tiers Fahrenheit at night. Luckily, winters are slight and short, proving distinctly tolerable for many.

Pack a few summery clothes even when journeying to Queen City at some stage in wintry weather; the weather is so unpredictable that travelers must prepare for anything.

Rental prices: $5 for a half of-hour bypass and $30 for a 24-hour bypass

Where To Eat In Charlotte

Charlotte's tourism extends to its culinary scene; the town has no scarcity of extremely good locations to consume, beginning with the Original Pancake House and finishing with drinks at Craft Tasting Room & Growler Shop.

For breakfast:

The Original Pancake House

This relaxed breakfast joint with two locations in midtown and South Park is most of the city's ideal alternatives for the day's first meal. Welcoming early morning clients, it serves warm and fresh meals to start the day, with services like salads, omelets, crêpes, and specialty pancakes.

Thanks to recipes which have been tried and tested for over two a long time, the bacon pancakes are specifically savory and a ought to-strive.

Address: 4736 Sharon Rd Sharon Corners Shopping Center, Charlotte, NC 28210-3328

Hours: Monday to Friday (6:30 am – 9 pm), Saturday & Sunday (7 am – nine pm)

For lunch and dinner:

Mama Ricotta's

Mama Ricotta's is a town classic that serves sumptuous Italian dishes. On the various menu, guests can order favorites like goat cheese and tomato basil sauce for the appetizer, followed via essential dishes, including own family-style pasta and New Haven-fashion pizzas. A veal marsala or chicken parmesan may be ideal for those feeling uncharacteristically ravenous.

Address: 601 S Kings Dr. AA, Charlotte, NC 28204-2932

Hours: Monday to Sunday (11 am – 9 pm)

Bar-B-Q King

Those with a gentle spot for vintage-style Southern traditional meals can head to Bar-B-Q King on Wilkinson Boulevard. Established in 1959, the joint has stood the check of time, supplying delicious servings of hickory-smoked barbecues, hen wings, sandwiches, and burgers. These include aspects of coleslaw and onion earrings or mac n cheese.

Address: 2900 Wilkinson Blvd, Charlotte, NC 28208-5624

Hours: Tuesday to Saturday (10:30 am – 10 pm)

For beverages:

Craft Tasting Room & Growler Shop

Featuring extra than 30 rotating beer faucets, bubbly, and a selection of wines, Craft Tasting Room has enough drinks to preserve the birthday celebration going late into the night. The joint particularly serves nearby beers for purchasers to attempt out the fresh taste from regional breweries like Suffolk Punch Brewing. A spacious patio within the bar is best for enjoying pints of beer at the same time as catching up with pals or mingling with the locals.

Address: 1320 S Church St, Charlotte, NC 28203

Hours: Monday to Wednesday (11 am – 10 pm), Thursday to Saturday (11 am-nighttime), Sunday (12 pm – 9 pm)

Make the most of the 7oz pours on Mondays for just $8.50, and strive Tuesday's $3 neighborhood pints.

Where to consume and drink in Charlotte.

Bar-B-Q King

Bar-B-Q King is a must-go to destination for any barbecue lover traveling Charlotte. It's been around when you consider that 1959, and that they've perfected their traditional southern recipes over the many years, with conventional fried chicken being one of their signature dishes. Their menu also boasts smoked pork, ribs, and other mouthwatering treats.

Dickey's Barbecue Pit

If you're searching out something a bit distinctive than conventional southern barbeque, Dickey's Barbecue Pit could be simply the factor. The first store opened in Dallas in 1941 and has been going robust ever considering, supplying Texas-fashion brisket that'll have your flavor buds tingling! It is one of the exceptional restaurants in Charlotte.

Fahrenheit

Fahrenheit is a high-quality desire for brunch. Enjoy stunning views from the rooftop patio as you tuck into a few traditional youth favorites together with pancakes and waffles – it's the proper start to your day! If you're looking for something extra high-priced then head to Sophia's Lounge at Ivey's Hotel in which you may revel in opulence stimulated via Queen Charlotte herself.

Halycon Restaurant

One of the most incredible Restaurants in Charlotte is the Haleycon Restaurant. Halycon is effortlessly positioned in South Tryon Street near more than one motel chains which include Embassy Suites, The Westin and The Hyatt Place Hotel.

Halycons is cherished both through local site visitors and nearby residents because of its artfully made selection of dishes like buckwheat burgers and cheese topped with neighborhood cheddar cheese. It makes sense for HalyCon to be voted one in every of Charlotte Observers' Best New Restaurants on the town for top notch food.

Firebirds Wood Fired Grill

A very common eating place in Charlotte would have to be a wooden fired firebird barbecue. Is the eating place appealing to those who've the maximum touchy flavor for meat or seafood? The majority of the menu objects are organized at the signature wooden grill imparting the first-class flavors and aromas. Contemporary décor accommodates open fireplaces, large wine racks and big bar collections.

Amelie's French Bakery

For travelers with a candy enamel, you want to visit Amelie's French Bakery. It has locations in which might be open 24/7, which means you could head there inside the small hours of the morning after a night time out! Their French inspired pastries and savories are successful among Charlotte natives.

NoDa Brewing Company

Charlotte is an area with dozens of breweries on its doorstep. Fans of craft beer might be of their detail. The NoDa Brewing Company offers IPAs, craft spiked seltzers and everything in between. They preserve everyday tours of the brewery, in addition to live tune.

Sugar Creek Brewing Company

Sugar Creek Brewing Company is placed on the lower south side of Charlotte. It creates a completely unique blend of Belgian-inspired ales that convey collectively modern flavor buds with conventional recipes to create a craft local beer this is growing a cult-following.

The Dilworth Tasting Room

Some of us decide on wine to craft beer. If you fall into this category, then you definately also have lots to discover in Charlotte. The Dilworth Tasting Room has an energetic social scene and sits in a Forties fashion constructing. You can sit down on the private patio or internal their wine bar. You can pattern European wine even as playing a cheese plate or the greater savory alternatives on their menu.

Cork buzz Restaurant and Wine Bar

If you need a few small plates together with your wine, then Cork buzz Restaurant and Wine Bar is your best spot in Charlotte. They run regular gives for the duration of the week, consisting of a half-price champagne discount at the weekends.

Ed's Tavern (Dilworth)

The famous community bar is an exquisite spot for drinking casually or dining. It is a popular place to play games or get the businesses collectively for a laugh trivialities. It's a swanky speakeasy with traditional cocktails and a traditional vibe. Started in Chapel Hill North Carolina and chose Charlotte as any other area. The meals is worth it, as are beverage & food! Excellent dinners and brunch additionally. Reservations are booked early so be organized for your arrival! Selwyn Pubs (Myers Park) – One of Myers Park's favored eating places recognized for its styro foam cups.

Where To Stay In Charlotte

Fountains and gardnes at First Ward Park, in Uptown Charlotte, North Carolina.

There is not any scarcity of accommodation regions within the Queen City, whether or not searching for a five-star suite within the coronary heart of Uptown with all the opulent services, an low-priced excursion apartment in one of the town's ancient suburbs, or an elaborate campsite inside the city's outskirts.

Luxury alternatives:

The Ritz-Carlton Charlotte

Address: 201 East Trade Street, Charlotte, NC 28202

Cost according to night time: Starts from $849 for 2 visitors

Amenities: Indoor pool, spa and well being middle, gymnasium, business center, restaurant, bar/living room, espresso store, free net, room provider, valet parking, flat-screen TV

The Ivey's Hotel

Address: 127 North Tryon Street, Charlotte, NC 28202

Cost consistent with night time: From $434

Amenities: City and atrium views, complimentary wine, fashionable rooms

Mid-variety options:

Grand Bohemian Hotel Charlotte Autograph Collection

Address: 201 West Trade Street, Charlotte, NC 28202

Cost in line with night: Starts from $309 for two guests

Amenities: Rooftop bar, in-house bar, pet-pleasant, chef-inspired catering, unfastened net, fitness center, room provider, unfastened toiletries, coffee device, satellite tv for pc, cable TV

Residence Inn by using Marriott Charlotte Uptown

Address: 404 South Mint Street, Charlotte, NC 28202

Cost in step with night: From $309

Amenities: Complimentary wine, hot breakfast, complimentary travel service, eating place & front room, secured (paid) parking

Budget alternatives:

Hilton Garden Inn Charlotte Airport

Address: 2400 Cascade Pointe Boulevard, Charlotte, NC 28208

Cost according to night time: Starts from $164 for 2 guests

Amenities: forty two-inch HDTV, complimentary Wi-Fi, separate residing place, complimentary health club, outside pool, fire pit, outside patio, unfastened breakfast, 24-hour pavilion pantry, front room, room service, complimentary 24-hour commercial enterprise center, assembly rooms

Best for households:

The Ballantyne, a Luxury Collection Hotel, Charlotte

Address: ten thousand Ballantyne Commons Parkway, Charlotte, NC 28277

Cost consistent with night: Starts from $382 for a family of 4

Amenities: Coffee machine, outdoor pool, gym, indoor pool, tea/coffee maker, room provider, spa and wellness middle, bar and lounge, complimentary Wi-Fi internet

Where to live in Charlotte

Uptown region is most popular neighborhoods for lodges. If you intend to go to Charlotte, that is the right area. Almost every appeal may be observed inside walking proximity.

Ballantyne gives upscale resorts from spa to tennis courts. There are many methods to relax in those regions. There is also the hazard to taste the maximum good sized whiskey collection in North Carolina and perhaps have lunch. P

The Best Hotels In Charlotte

The Ballantyne

The Ballantyne is a luxury motel that offers the entirety from a spa to tennis courts. It's the ideal spot to go to unwind and loosen up. You can sample one of the most important whiskey collections in North Carolina and even bask in a day tea. The inn gives a complimentary shuttle across the local region to get you to and points of interest. With The Ballantyne, you could experience each indoor and outdoor swimming pools

The Westin

If you're touring for a sport on the Stadium of Bank of America, or for an occasion on the Convention Centre, then the Westin is a tremendous lodge to stay in. You can relax within the tranquility of the hotel rooms that provide Westin's 'Heavenly' beds. The lodge has a fitness studio, numerous eating places, a café that serves Starbucks and 24-hour room provider. The Westin is also a pet-pleasant inn in case you want to deliver alongside your four-legged pal.

Charlotte Marriott City Centre

For tourists who want the convince of being inside the city center, the Marriott is a first-rate choice of motel. You're within taking walks distance of the

Bank of America Stadium, and you may easily bounce into an Uber to visit other areas of the city. Their restaurant, Stoke, offers a menu complete of Southern delicacies. If you want to work all through your experience, you may visit their Event Hub.

Embassy Suites by means of Hilton Charlotte, Uptown

With this resort, you're as close to the Spectrum Centre as you can get. You also have a Whole Foods simply next door. You'll also be inside strolling distance of the NASCAR Hall of Fame. If you're searching out the benefit of someplace that's in the middle of the motion, then this hotel is a really perfect spot.

Your stay includes a loose breakfast and complimentary night reception with free snacks and beverages. You can experience perspectives of the Charlotte skyline from the terrace of this resort even as taking part in a pitcher of your preferred wine.

Holiday Inn Charlotte Centre City

The Holiday Inn is a finances-pleasant option in Uptown Charlotte. You'll be right in the middle of Charlotte, with the Mint Museum on the doorstep. This hotel is 8 miles faraway from the airport and has the Spectrum Arena as it's neighbor. If you're bringing your youngsters alongside, then remarkable news! Kids below 18 get to stay without spending a dime when sharing a room with a parent.

CHAPTER 3: BEST NEIGHBORHOODS IN AND AROUND CHARLOTTE

Charlotte, North Carolina, USA uptown lit up skyline and park.

Can't determine wherein to live in Charlotte? Queen City boasts a handful of old fashioned neighborhoods and districts.

Uptown

While downtown is the norm when describing the city middle in maximum towns, Charlotteans go in opposition to the grain in relating to their urban center as Uptown. This busy economic district by using day transforms right into a energetic nightlife spot beneath the quilt of darkness.

The location is rife with stores, boutiques, eating places, and other companies. The historical buildings that once stood there have considering been converted into luxury condos but maximum of Charlotte's museums can be found in Uptown.

NoDa

NoDa, an acronym for North Davidson, is the town's historic arts district and houses many old fashioned art galleries, overall performance theaters, and live track venues. Not too a long way away, visitors will come across an emerging neighborhood called Plaza Midwood. The vicinity is home to iconic local restaurants like Dish and The Penguin.

Myer's Park

Situated a few blocks from Charlotte's Uptown, Myer's Park is the oldest suburb in the town and is described with the aid of the excellent houses in town. The atmosphere is comfy and tranquil, marked with tree-covered streets and plush greenery, and perfect for a laid-again nighttime stroll.

Here, vacationers can excursion the city's nice locations of worship, which include Myers Park Methodist Church and the Little Church at the Lane.

University City

This neighborhood is predominantly occupied by using college students from exclusive campuses within the city. As such, the nightlife is loopy, with sports activities bars and pubs welcoming a younger crowd at night. The vicinity additionally hosts an awesome number of Fortune 500 business enterprise campuses.

Matthews

Mathews is a small city bordering the city and a part of Mecklenburg County. The charming suburb hosts a active farmer's market on Saturday, really worth visiting to pattern the fresh neighborhood produce and different products. Cycling lovers can also take at the Four Mile Creek Greenway, a amusing out of doors interest out of doors the city.

Tips for Visiting Charlotte

Distance signs and symptoms at The Green, in Uptown Charlotte, North Carolina.

Charlotte is the second one-biggest of the Southeastern towns after Jacksonville, FL, and among America's top ten fastest-growing cities. Its populace, at just below 900,000, is the 16th largest in the united states, made from a friendly network displaying Southern hospitality at its greatest.

The metropolis enjoys a booming financial system spurred with the aid of banking, technology, and manufacturing companies. Several Fortune 500 groups, inclusive of Bank of America, Nucor, and Duke Energy, are established in Charlotte.

Founded in 1799, the town turned into dubbed the Queen City after Charlotte of Mecklenburg-Strelitz, the queen consort of King George the 3rd at some point of the metropolis's founding. Charlotte is also credited with kicking off the Carolina Gold Rush when a teenage boy ran into the u . S . A .'s first gold nugget.

Queen City lies in a damp subtropical climate comprising 4 awesome seasons. The usually temperate weather is best for exploring the outside year-round, despite the fact that it can be pretty unpredictable. It's no longer uncommon for a sunny summer season day to have a torrential downpour.

Outdoor adventurers will get a kick out of Charlotte as the town is synonymous with inexperienced spaces. With over forty miles of greenbelt belongings in place and plans to expand a further one hundred+ miles, open areas, strolling paths, and biking trails dominate here.

Sports also are a huge deal in Queen City, which hosts a handful of professional sports franchises and different groups inside the minor leagues. Catching a game is one of the maximum interesting things to do in Charlotte.

The Carolina Panthers of the NFL are the town's pride, and this is genuine for the Charlotte Hornets (NBA) and Charlotte FC (MLS). Also, NASCAR has appreciably stimulated the city's persona, with Charlotte website hosting the NASCAR Hall of Fame and staging races on the Charlotte Motor Speedway.

How To Spend The Perfect Day In Charlotte

Graham Library and grounds, Charlotte, North Carolina,

Begin the day with breakfast at The Original Pancake House earlier than embarking at the city's ancient tour at Levine Museum of the New South. Scan and explore the permanent exhibits, inclusive of the treasured "Cotton Fields to Skyscrapers" show.

Move to the Charlotte Museum of History for extra on the town's past, then head to the Levine Center for Arts to check out the three museums inside it.

After admiring the loads of pieces from renowned artists like Pablo Picasso and Alberto Giacometti, take a taxi to Mama Ricottas for an true Italian lunch. Later, hit the 7th Street Public Market to experience a pitcher of freshly squeezed fruit juice and experience a flavor of what North Carolina's popular farmer's markets provide.

Spend the early afternoon at Daniel Stowe Botanical Garden, then a ride to the U.S. National Whitewater Center. With more than enough a laugh at the center to remaining the whole afternoon, be sure to go away simply in time to seize a Southern-style supper at Haberdish within the NoDa community.

Cap the time without work with a pint of neighborhood craft beer at Craft Tasting Room &

Growler Shop at the same time as mingling with different revelers late into the night.

Whether you are a beer buff, a sports activities fan, or into the arts scene, you'll discover some thing to love all through a go to Charlotte, North Carolina, a vibrant metropolis inside the Piedmont region close to the South Carolina border. Here are some of the Queen City's ought to-see spots to add to the itinerary in your subsequent experience.

Culture And Arts

Appreciate Art At Mint Museum Uptown

Uptown Charlotte is domestic to several museums all inside an easy walk of each other. Stop via the Mint Museum, North Carolina's first art museum, to revel in famous on cutting-edge and historic artwork, decorative arts, and layout. Several large public sculptures mounted round city also are controlled by way of Mint.

See 'The Firebird' At Bechtler Museum of Modern Art

From the Mint Museum, you could take a short stroll to the Bechtler Museum of Modern Art. A 17-foot French mosaic sculpture, "The Firebird," presides over the welcome plaza. The museum become designed via a Swiss architect and holds the gathering of Bessie and Hans Bechtler. You can see works via Pablo Picasso, Andy Warhol, and many other 20th-century artists.

Expand Horizons At Harvey B. Gantt Center For African-American Arts + Culture

Visit the Harvey B. Gantt Center for African-American Arts + Culture, named for the nearby trailblazer who was Charlotte's first African-American mayor. Admire the permanent collection of African-American and Haitian art as well as travelling reveals, which regularly function modern-day artists.

Entertain The Kids At Discovery Place

Those with little tourists in tow need to add a visit to Discovery Place to the itinerary. The hands-on technological know-how museum is equal components amusing and academic. Labs, stay shows, and IMAX films upload to the instructional revel in.

Activities For Sports Fans

Catch A Charlotte Knights Game

Visiting throughout baseball season? Make sure to capture a Charlotte Knights sport. Truist Field, domestic of the Triple-A Charlotte Knights, became these days voted the Best Ballpark in Minor League

Baseball, and for top cause. It's a terrifi vicinity to revel in America's pastime.

Visit The NASCAR Hall Of Fame

NASCAR fans will want to make a pit prevent at the NASCAR Hall of Fame in Uptown. Interactive exhibits file the records of NASCAR within the Hall of Fame, which additionally honors the legends in the sport. Major lovers can time their visit with an induction and spot stars walk the red carpet.

Go Whitewater Rafting

For folks who are extra into outside sports, there are few places extra enticing than the U.S. National Whitewater Center. The Center is home to the biggest guy-made whitewater river within the international. With 1,300 acres of land and extra than 50 miles of trails, there is masses of room to hike, bike, or try your hand at standup paddle boarding.

Where To Shop

Stop At Boutiques In South End

No experience is entire without a little retail therapy, and Charlotte's South End community is a first-rate area to start, wherein possibilities to keep neighborhood abound. Visit the Girl Tribe flagship store for cheeky shirts, accessories, home items, and extra, all with an emphasis on female empowerment.

Then, take hold of an ultra-cozy, nostalgia-stimulated t-blouse, beanie, or sweatshirt at Glory Days Apparel. You'll discover lots of Charlotte-branded equipment to permit all of us understand you paid the Queen City a go to. Add some sparkle in your look with rings from The Golden Carrot.

Sophisticated gents can time table a custom becoming or just keep at Ole Mason Jar, that is positioned within the Design Center of the Carolinas. Not quite positive what you're looking for? Drop by using Charlotte Collective. The area houses products from extra than a dozen local makers multi function spot, making it clean to browse.

Stroll Through Dilworth

Check out the stores in Dilworth, a historical community acknowledged for walkable, tree-covered streets, eateries, and wine bars. Paper Skyscraper is an independently owned present shop packed with unique items which include delicious candles, fun books, and hostess items she'll without a doubt use. Vestique is a designer apparel boutique that prides itself on finding lower priced, on-trend models.

CHAPTER 4: TOP ACTIVITIES – FUN THINGS TO DO IN CHARLOTTE

Visit the South End Neighborhood

The South End neighborhood of Charlotte is a trendy region full of cute boutiques, restaurants and cafes. There also are many amusing work of art and this is a awesome area to test out avenue art.

Walking around this neighborhood you'll also find many breweries and bars, and they're a brilliant area for an evening out.

While in South End be sure to test out Pepperbox Doughnuts and Jeni's Splendid Ice Creams – they're each delicious treats!

To get to South End from Uptown Charlotte you may take the tram or force 5ish minutes (1.5 miles). If you have time, you can additionally easily walk!

Check Out Optimist Hall

Optimist Hall is a stunning food corridor positioned about 5 minutes through automobile (1.Five miles) from Uptown Charlotte.

Optimist Hall has tons of extraordinary meals options – with the entirety from ramen and bao to empanadas and tacos. Everything seemed so top that it become extraordinarily hard to pick wherein to consume!

In addition to all of the yummy meals, there also are heaps of indoor and out of doors seating areas. You can include pals to revel in a meal, or deliver your laptop to get a few paintings executed at the same time as playing a espresso (or a cocktail!)

Any time of day, breakfast, lunch or dinner, you're positive to discover some thing delicious to devour.

Explore Uptown Charlotte

The metropolis center of Charlotte is the Uptown community. This is in which you'll locate museums, restaurants, bars and plenty of company offices.

Uptown Charlotte, despite being the metropolis middle, is fairly small and effortlessly walkable! To begin your day,I recommend grabbing a coffee and heading to The Green, a small park at once across from the Mint Museum and Bechtler Museum of Modern Art.

The Mint Museum

The Mint Museum is a four floor museum full of galleries! The Mint Museum has several artwork reveals on display, ranging from style to modern artwork to sculptures.

You can effortlessly spend a pair hours wandering around this museum and viewing the art on display!

Tickets to the museum are $15 for adults and $10 for teachers, students and seniors.

Bechtler Museum of Modern Art

Located just round the corner to the Mint Museum, the Bechtler Museum of Modern Art is also worth a visit.

The museum is pretty small, so you can easily see all the famous in an hour or so.

Tickets to the museum are $9 for adults and $7 for college kids and seniors.

Take a City Tour with Queen City Rides

If you're interested in getting to know approximately Charlotte, its landmarks and its history, this is a exquisite excursion for you!

Book tickets on the Queen City golf cart and journey across the city to peer and listen approximately most of the most important sites!

Tours are 1.5 hours long and are offered at a couple of times during the day.

Take a Ghost Tour

Personally, I assume that this is one of the great activities in Uptown Charlotte!

Although Charlotte probably isn't the primary location that comes to thoughts while you think of ghosts or haunted cities, it's loads spookier than you think! Uptown Charlotte, particularly, has a darkish beyond that has brought about a ghost crammed present.

On your ghost tour you'll find out about the gold rush in Charlotte, the collapsed mines, and the ghosts that still inhabit the ancient homes and agencies inside the metropolis.

This is a brilliant way to spend your nighttime!

The Weekend Guide: Public Art, Fried Chicken, and White Water Rafting in Charlotte

Charlotte, North Carolina, has an established recognition as a nearby banking center, however in case you're still brushing off it as a town constructed around business lunches, you're manner behind. In the past decade, Charlotte's one of a kind neighborhoods, entrepreneurial spirit, and food (and beer and cocktail) scene have come to the fore. As workplaces reopen in employee-friendly Uptown, the metropolis is ready to get returned to enterprise. Here's our plan for a full Charlotte weekend.

Day 1

Wake up at the Grand Bohemian, the town's maximum fashionable, artwork-packed new inn, that is centrally positioned inside the Uptown commercial enterprise district. Walk a few blocks for brunch at The Asbury, inside the lobby of the Dunhill Hotel; don't sleep on the sticky biscuits, pinwheels rolled with united states ham and drizzled with goat cheese icing.

Take your select of close by museums, which include the Harvey B. Gantt Center for African-American Arts + Culture, the Mint Museum Uptown and its notable crafts collection, and the Bechtler Museum of Modern Art—Niki de Saint-Phalle's reflected Firebird is a popular image spot. Next, wander via Romare Bearden Park, an homage to the Charlotte-born artist respected for his collages of Black lifestyles in the South.

Stop by way of 7th Street Public Market, an incubator for nearby meals companies together with Orrman's Cheese Shop and Assorted Table Wine Shoppe; then hop at the Lynx light rail line to NoDa, the North Davidson Street arts district.

The artwork-filled lobby at the Grand Bohemian inn

Once there, attempt the updated Southern cooking (assume seriously crispy hushpuppies with sweet tea butter) at Haberdish, in which salvaged-denim cubicles don't forget the location's fabric-mill history. Next, browse through NoDa's small stores and galleries, such as Pura Vida Worldly Art and the Rat's Nest, with its vintage Western and '70s garb.

Rio, Off the Beach

Finish your day with a have a look at how Charlotte has been revitalizing its old business spaces. Camp North End—the site of a 1924 Ford manufacturing unit and Cold War–generation missile plant—is a steampunk dream. Here, you'll discover Leah & Louise, a modern take on a Memphis juke joint, wherein Greg and Subrina Collier reinterpret dishes born in the Mississippi River Valley, such as candy-and-spicy bird skins fried to a potato chip–like crisp and roasted cabbage swimming in a rich pork-neck bisque.

Day 2

Begin your morning with a 5-minute ride to the South End warehouse district, and fuel up with the lemon ricotta pancakes at Lincoln's Haberdashery, a aggregate bakery, coffeehouse, and market in an old Lance Cracker manufacturing unit.

Next, stroll the Charlotte Rail Trail, a extensive path along the light rail line that's dotted with public artwork, together with "magic carpets" painted without delay at the pavement. On Saturday mornings, prevent into the South End Market to choose up locally grown greens or Ekologicall's zero-waste domestic merchandise. On your stroll returned north, hop off the path for lunch at the almost six-decade-vintage Price's Chicken Coop, which is famous for its fried fowl and killer gizzards. It's blue-collar and takeout best, with carrier that is brusque however pleasant.

Camp North End, a meals hall constructed in a 1924 Ford plant

Breweries have popped up throughout Charlotte, with seven in the South End alone. At Sycamore Brewing, revel in a Southern Girl Blonde at the expansive outside patio. If you're not a lager drinker, sample the sophisticated ginger ale—which has greater chew than sweetness—on the rooftop on the Unknown Brewing Company, overlooking Bank of America Stadium.

For dinner, head to the Elizabeth neighborhood, with its Craftsman-style charm that dates to the 1920s. Start with a Gin Gin Mule—a mashup of a mojito and a Moscow mule—at The Crunkleton; it's a private membership, which means you'll want to stable a $10 annual club whilst you make a reservation. Next door is The Stanley, wherein James Beard Award semifinalist Paul Verica crafts innovative seasonal plates, like a crispy kale version of a conventional frisée salad with a poached egg. Or switch them: The Crunkleton has stay-fireplace cooking, and The Stanley has fantastic cocktails.

Day 3

You have an lively day beforehand, so set out early for a quick breakfast inside the Belmont community at Optimist Hall, a popular food hall in a former fabric mill. Try Undercurrent Coffee for a golden milk latte and tricked-out avocado toast or overnight oatmeal.

For a morning of adventure, force 20 minutes west to the U.S. National Whitewater Center, which occupies 1,3 hundred acres along the Catawba River, together with the world's largest synthetic white water river. You can buy an afternoon pass or choose person activities, which include white- and flat-water kayaking, rafting, ziplining, and mountain cycling. Some activities are seasonal, so take a look at the every day agenda earlier than you go.

Head again to Plaza-Midwood, a various and busy 1950s-era business district. At Dish, a diner with a homestyle vibe, take your choose from Southern classics, like deviled eggs, extraordinary biscuits, and hen and dumplings.

Steakhouse-inspired Southern delicacies at Supperland

To get a sense of the neighborhood's energy, stroll past the Thirsty Beaver Saloon. The popular dive bar and tune club refused to promote out to developers, so builders wrapped an condo constructing round it. Continue exploring Central Avenue and stop into boutiques like Cltch, which sells vintage accessories, barware, and dad-lifestyle merchandise.

Dinner this night is at one of Plaza-Midwood's maximum thrilling new restaurants, Supperland, located in a renovated 1950s church. Thoughtful decor consists of their very own line of dishware covered with dogwood, sweet potato, and squash blossom designs, whilst the menu draws inspiration from both steakhouses (entrees like high ribeye and spatchcocked branzino) and church potlucks (assume "franks and beans" made with Wagyu hot puppies and Sea Island crimson peas). Bar master Colleen Hughes has been given a separate area within the antique church annex, where she's turning out clever cocktails with touches like rose-formed ice edged with glitter in order to stop your visit on a boozy excessive.

FAQ

Is Charlotte worth journeying?

Charlotte is a lovely town for touring due to its ancient homes and its southern allure. There is lots of amusing and amusement to attend whether it's miles a circle of relatives holiday, a wedding excursion or a own family occasion. This town deserves the visit!

How many days must in Charlotte ?

It takes three days to vacation in Charlotte. It affords you a good risk to find out numerous neighborhoods and get an excellent evaluate of every detail in the metropolis. It's clean to increase your trip to three days of journey.

What is Charlotte most known for?

Charlotte is known its sports activities team the Carolina's Panthers of the NFL and the Charlotte Hornets NBA Team. There are lots of different points of interest inclusive of numerous universities, expert faculties and universities. It is likewise the 17th maximum populous metropolis inside the country and the North Carolina's biggest town.

Where should I stay in Charlotte?

The excellent component about Charlotte's neighborhoods is that the neighborhoods generally tend to have character personalities. You can enjoy Uptown at the weekends and weekdays (FYI – downtown Charlotte may be known as Uptown Charlotte). If you extend your location past ten or twenty miles you can discover picturesque lakes towns, outdoor retreats, university lifestyles and greater.

How to Save Money in Charlotte, North Carolina?

Check the tourist web site for specials. Visit Charlotte offers reductions and gives on each enchantment and motel on its web page. Plan a summer season holiday in Queen City. Summers are warm and bustling, and resort rates are high. You could make your travels a touch bit cheaper for the duration of wintry weather months. Avoid a overdue-night ride to the resort.

Is Charlotte Safe?

Alright, and now it's time in this Charlotte tour manual to address some commonplace questions oldsters may have when contemplating travelling

Queen City: Is Charlotte safe?

Personally, Charlotte felt safe to me, in particular for the duration of the day. It is a town, in order constantly hold your commonplace wits about you. I noticed the South End neighborhood became properly-lit at night with different young (and young-at-coronary heart) residents strolling about, so I felt outstanding comfortable hanging out there after dinner while we strolled around for dessert. South End is likewise superb for bar hopping (as mentioned earlier in my Charlotte travel guide), so

I'd advise that location for a few past due-night time a laugh.

Printed in Great Britain
by Amazon

38237144R00035